Just a Snowy Scene

One Hundred Poems

By

Ray Lee

Contents

Just a Snowy Scene 9

Station 10

Hen 12

Just the One 13

Skylark 14

The Right Image 16

Autumn Sun 17

Autumn 18

The Fishing Party	19
Redbrick Sprawl	20
Fish	21
Lazy Day	22
Traitor	24
Loneliness	25
Last Autumn	26
First Impressions	27
Sudden Change	28
Hiroshima	30
Disco Dancing	32
Mist	34
The Long Wait	36
Recollections	37
Fingers on a Wall Top	38
Pub	39
The Cinema	40
Tree	42
Just A Reminder	43

Garden	43
Time	46
Stricken Tree	47
I Used to Do It	48
Harvest	50
Park	52
Door	53
Ripe	54
Really	55
An Idea Jam	56
Mill	58
Buzzard	60
The Second Coming	61
Need	62
Riverbank	63
Suppose	64
Raindrop	66
Daydream	68
Swallow	69

Kestrel 70

Alone 71

Possibility 72

Oldness 73

If 74

Bright Eyed Fox 76

Another Swallow 77

Footsteps 77

Idle Moment 79

Love 80

Autumn Snapshot 81

Owls 82

Starling 83

Peacetalk 84

Viaduct 86

Removal Day 88

Tarn 90

Dawn Realisation 91

Shoes 92

How Irrational	93
The Gala	94
It Was an Instant	96
Raging	97
One Step Further	98
Firebird	99
Approaching Storm	100
A Sudden Gust	102
Heron	103
Anger	104
Stormy Jackdaw	105
Brief Encounter	106
Bird On a Rock	108
The Nettle	110
What Is It	112
Yesterday	113
A Giggle of Water	114
The Ruthless Water	115
Spider	116

Funny	117
Glorious	118
Oyster Catcher	120
Leaf Fall	121
In The Footsteps	122
The Grey Room	124
Seascape	126
Bean Sprout	127
The Autumn Wind	128
Sense Of Direction	130
The Power Shovel	132
Things	134
Ninth Symphony	136
The Dance	138
Meteor	140
A Moment of Peace	141

This book is dedicated to my lovely wife Jenny who took this photograph.

Just a Snowy Scene

In this wood
There are no leaves
On the trees.
Last year's crop lies
Rotting beneath the
Smudged
Snow.
Trees
Creaking
And
Complaining
Of
The wind
Shake
Like shivering
Bones.
Yet
Safe in silence
Caught and curled
Budded life
Waits.

Station

Broken panes apart
From a distance
It still looks proud
But as you approach it
Distress
Increases.
Windows
Like dimmed eye sockets
Weep at the touching stones.
Inside
Ceilings hang in carious shreds
And reveal, a roof
Open to the sky.
An office door
Clings crookedly
By a single hinge,
Panels,
Long beaten
Move
Pining in the wind.

Underfoot
Glass crackles.
Smashed reflections
Glint from dark crevices.
A broken pipe
Juts
From rain rotted timber.
Once it supported a lamp
Whose light
Hissed
Brightened
And dimmed
Like a flux of dying breath.

Hen

Although the sky was
Cloudless and calm,
The sun soothing
And sympathetic,
The summerhouse peaceful,
My discontent was septic.
My foot without several toes
Ached with the continuity
Of Schoenberg.
A disjointed thrum, thrum
And bloody thrum.
Who could sleep to that rhythm?
Then she came with red feathers
Glowing
A soft throaty hypnotic chuckle
Expressing her contentment.
To my surprise she settled on the grass
And continued to
Fuss her ticking call gently
Until I slept.

Just the One

At first
The thought
Of one hand clapping
Is preposterous.
But
If you shut your eyes
You can see it beating
In the darkness.
If you imagine
A sudden
Shuddering stop
And a silent
Percussion
The applause
Grows to a thundering roar
Which is sufficient
To keep you awake at night.
Go on try it.
If you can imagine one hand
The rest is
Easy.

Skylark

Blueness is devoured
In electric silence.
A skylark
Rising to hover
Like a full stop
Punctuating a sheet of blue
Is smudged into murky cloud,
Its song is blotted.
Trees
Once a vigorous outline
Of black and green
Are like fine features
Viewed through a veil.
Rain
With hissing haste
Blisters the fellside.
Earth
Hurls up a fragrance
Of rain
And dry mud.

The skylark,
Hushed,
Plummets
To shelter
As best it can
In drenched trash.

The Right Image

Someone said to me
A man's tidiness
Is an expression
Of the kind of person he is.
It would be easy to agree
If that's your disposition
But think
Of the unkempt Christ
Walking from the wilderness
On holy sandals to the garden
And of the jackbooted generals
Whose creases
Were as ordered
As their filing cabinet minds.
Think
How neatly
They kept their souvenirs
Right down
To the last flake
Of skin.

Autumn Sun

The sun gushed
Light
Filling the world with gold.
It hung on
Longer into the evening
Than expected.
Then
As if its strength
Had finally given,
It seemed to drop
Like a vast shimmering stone
Into the further valley.

Autumn

Clouds
Were as grey as limestone,
Depressing as pollution.
My leaden steps loitered
In the dawdling drizzle.
But then I saw the leaves,
No longer sodden brown
They moved on the air
Like dancers
In a wild whirling ballet.
A riotous choreography
Twirling
Red
Orange
Gold
Yellow.
Abruptly
My heart joined in
Singing
As I was blown along.

The Fishing Party

Child
Dead
In the water.
Interested groups
Watch
The fishing party.
I suppose
They would be insulted
If I invited them
To finger his dead flesh
Or suggest they linger
To savour
The stench of decomposition.
What!
On holiday!
They would whinge.

Redbrick Sprawl

Redbrick
Sprawl,
Once
The best end of the estate.
Dawn.
The air is ripe
With dust
And steamy mongrel smells.
Doors
Once grained and polished
Shed faded lacquers
Like tired skin.
Windows in fragile frames
Are blind.
Inside the houses
Inhabitants persist.
The maggots
Rot
With the apple.

Fish

Gleaming
In the sunshine
Glittering fish
Rainbowed
and delightful
Hide your brilliance
Under a slimy stone
For the fishermen
Is coming
With his cruel hook.

Lazy Day

It's a lazy day.
The long-haired black cow
Suckles her curly calf.
It slobbers
At her gleaming teats
And milk beards
It's extremely clean mouth.
Hens
Scrabble and scratch
In the spinning jewels of dust
To rid themselves of fleas.
Then they stretch
Ridiculous sunbathers
And lay out
Their flat
Hot
Brown wings
To the sun.
Yellow
Needle like flowers
Of Good King Henry
Fleck
Their half - opened beaks.

One broody bird
Spreads her wings
Like a freckled parasol
To hide her chicks,
And slowly backs away
Making gentle
Throaty
Clucking sounds
As she goes.

Traitor

How the blood.
Must flow like mucous
In your polluted brain.
How life's exchange
Has robbed you
Of even the decency
Of a simple petal.
Life's real bouquets
Of pain and joy will
Never be yours.
Your world
Is like a tight curled bud
Blighted
Never to open
And savour
The sun's true light.

Loneliness

In the poor man's
Quarter of the city
The gardens were fleshy
And thigh deep with weeds.
The green door
To the house
Was puckered and blistered
Just like his life.
It was dark
And he was alone.
Membrane walls
Diffused
Brick muted laughter.
A placard
Painted with cliches
Leant against the wall.
Rain tapped
A tap dripped
A clock
Ticked.

Last Autumn

A season
Brown as a muddy puddle.
Fog
Sucked lungs
Like drawn boils.
Stiff sheets
And a fire crackled
In the grate.
Days
Upon days
When pain flared
And spirits flickered
With the frailty
Of a flowering
Candle.

First Impressions

Through the door she came
Black velvet and copper.
Just one look
Was a moment like a priest's
First fondle.
Only seconds
Separated this thought
From the idea
Of my child
Rumpling her belly skin.
As I turned to go
I heard a crash of books.
As I picked up
The crop of fallen pages
I raised my head
And found it near her loins.
I was as close as Judas
When Christ knew
The kiss was inevitable.
Using the bookshelves
As support
I pulled myself upright.
Thanks
She said.

Sudden Change

Time
Dripped
Throughout the wet autumn.
Slimy leathery leaves
Blocked runnels and door bottoms.
Wind
Drove water
At the farmhouse walls
Day after day after day.
Water
Sang in the drainpipes
And splattered
Against the clogged ground.
In a frenzy
Ash twigs
Dipped
Flicked
Battered and tapped.
Mud,
Rich
Luxurious
Boot sucking mud,
Filled the farmyard.

Life coughed
Plumes of steamy breath
In regular anxious bursts.
When the change came
It came suddenly.
We awoke
To find our breath
Steaming
In the ice-cold bedroom.
Our counterpane
Stiff with frozen condensation.
It was the silence
That amazed us
After the lashing
Nagging music
Of the past weeks.
It seemed as unnatural
As a dead smile.
Frost
Had gripped the dale
With a god's grasp
And all the windows
Had delicately
Blossomed
To worship him.

Hiroshima

The day
Was as peaceful
As a jay's wing is blue
When
Out of the ceramic sapphire sky
The low drone
Bee noise began.
On the streets
People
Tended their lives
Like banked up fires
Easy
In their occasional flames.
The noise grew
As the dragon came
To deliver dawn.
People barely moved
As the fire vaporised
Even scorched stone to ash.

Then came the roar,
Splintering pane and drum
For a hundred miles
And the whole world
Was instantly silenced.
Voiceless wind
Drove the dragon's mischief
Into every raw place
Until finally it rained
And rained and rained
Black rain
Black sorrow.

Disco Dancing

The rain
Beat on the pavement
Like breaking beads
But going in was difficult.
It was as though
All unentered rooms
Contained the carrion
Of someone abandoned
Among extreme tidiness.
I nudged the door.
A solid wind of sound
Pressed my ribcage.
On the dancefloor
A lattice of limbs
Throbbed
Twitching independently
Yet bonded to a whole
Like scintillating atoms
Vibrating in a crystal.
It was easy
To remain detached
Among such activity.

It was easy
To survive on fantasy
But her body
Was equally lovely
By red light
Blue yellow orange
And quaking green.

Mist

I am
A living tissue
Shivering
On a bleak bone.
Mist
Like a soggy poultice
Clings.
Trees lurk
In sodden seclusion
Slowly
Gathering
From gloom
Like prodigal brothers
Searching.
Leaves flicker
Indecisively.
Nearby
A bird calls
Its voice dead
Among semi-permeable dampness.

Mist
Swirls angrily from my path
Only to close
With pernicious stealth
Behind me.

The Long Wait

Hunting.
An ancient pursuit.
Urged on by libido and brown ale
I waited and
Waited.
Then the rain stopped.
A car
Hissed through a puddle
Spraying black droplets
Into the air.
They burst like yellow
Chrysanthemums
On
The
Road.

Recollections

In a warmed cupboard
Ironed starch
Smelled like cornflowers.
Under the shelf
He flew
His spitfire.
Father said,
A friend had died,
Broken by war.
The boy fingered
A bear with a split back
And wondered.
He knew that father hated Germans,
Killers of men who loan money
And of babies.
Babies
And bayonet tennis pricked his sleep.
What protection was a blanket
Should God
After all be German.

Fingers on a Wall

Fingers
Fumbled
The wall top.
Such an effort to see
Vegetables
Coiled
Tight as new ideas
And
Roses big as a face.
How slowly flowers
Bloomed
And
Died
And
Bruised petals fell
Then.

Pub

Glasses slithered
And clonked
On a tray.
The busy bottomed barmaid
Brushed past me
And smiled
Knowingly.
You can still write poems
You can still
Find a bit of crumpet
And live off her.
The voice fascinated
And
Charmed conscience
Like a snake
From a basket.

The Cinema

Under the cinema hoarding
Green lights shone.
A bloated breasted woman
Who was about to be initiated
Into the vampire society
Had
Coming shortly
Plastered
Where her knickers
Should have been.
My feet ached with the cold.
I knew it was eight o'clock
Yet dare not
Look at my watch.
During the time I had waited
People
Had met
People had parted
With as little fuss
As a flower opening.
But then she came.
In the treacly dark
We felt our way
To the remotest corner.

Bliss.
Until the light returned
And we saw the chaos.
Flakes of paper
Blobs of paint
Dusty Handprints
On her dress.
Black patches
Where patches shouldn't be.
Rising
Straightening
Hitching up
Levelling down
Pushing past
All in one precise flow.
Outside
An old man
In a plum coloured uniform
Came
And pasted
Twice nightly
Over
Coming shortly.

Tree

Her sap sticky lips
Moved against mine
And my hand
Found hair
As course as sun warmed sand.
Her body had the resilience
Of a sapling
Playing the wind.
My face
Sighed amongst fleshy fruits
And we moaned
As though a wind
Tore the branches.
Soon
We lay as still
As a single seed.

Just A Reminder

Orange
To pale ragged yellow
To blistered hoary
white
The dissolving sun
Spreads
Uncertain shadows
Behind me.
My own dwindling
Image
Stretches
Forever further
And
Fainter
Relating
To the inconsequential
Fragility
Of being
And self.

Garden

The place my garden
Often lives
Is somewhere in my head.
The shape of it
Clear as an acid
Etching
Stark in its relief.
Images sprout with clarity.
I see bees
Raiding the foxgloves
And hear
The music of a blackbird
Pulsing
Like the scintillations
And pauses
Of a Beethoven quartet.
Gently
The sweet peas
Share their sweetness
Subtly infiltrating the air
As the thrush
Dances and darts
Joy in its stamping claws
As it provokes its prey.

The grass is always there
As green as a fugue
If only I could sing it
And rival the robin
Whose breast
Outshines the roses.
Even the old shed
Is dignified
As it changes
Its shades of drifting brown
In the vagrant sunlight
Which threads
The nearby branches.

Time

As I lay
In bed under the blue
Dull lighted
Nine o'clock moon
The sheets are uncomfortable
Like corrugated card.
Time
Moves like a dray cart
Dragged by a glue bound horse.
I think of those outside
Who will see
How the early evening moon
Scintillates
Among leaf fall hair.
I wish
It was autumn
For me again.

.

Stricken Tree

It was evening
And sticky hot.
The sky
Bruised silver
Dulled
As suddenly
The moon became
Hooded in cloud
And vanished
Like an owl's eye.
Lightning lashed
Hissing and mocking
The treetops
As if with wild laughter.
One tree shimmered
Green and orange
As fire slowly
Peeled to the ground
Where soil
Flicked and sprayed
Into the air
Only To fall
rhythmically
Like brown rain.

I Used to Do It

But that was
Before
My eyes went.
The field was green
Was all I could say
With certainty
Without my jam-jar bottoms.
A voice made words
But the face
Was so far above me
I had to squint
To recognise any features.
He cantered off.
Somewhere
In the distance
A whistle bleated
Flump
The ball came within my field of vision
But
Too quickly for me to avoid it.

Which bent most
Ball or head.
This question
Like the existence of God
Or any other bland
Philosophical issue
Will remain debatable.
The ball
Remained part of the match
I didn't.

Harvest

Raising his head
To the wind
The boy sniffed the fat air
Which was damp
As the atmosphere
Craved the relief of
Rain.
Throughout the meadow
The tractor threaded the hay.
His arms prickled and smarted
And ached
As he rolled pushed and pulled
Bails
As heavy as himself.
At last
He was reached for
And flipped to the load top
Where he lay
Laughing
Stacked under the beaten sky.
Down the road
The load swayed.
He lay still
Too breathless to speak.

As branches
Flicked by
The first blisters of rain stung.
Lightning crackled.
The tops of the trees
Purpled.
Thunder tumbled.
The bull
Restless in the field
Stamped his hooves
And called the cows.
It was as though
The great god bull
Was rising
To the taunt of the hammer
In the Viking dale
Of long ago.

Park

Getting up
I saw the park
Shift and stumble.
Crows
In the nearby trees
Disturbed
By sudden movement
Clattered
Into the air.
Through the nearby
windows
Flames trembled
Like joyful fingers.
You should always
Be made love to
By firelight
I thought.

Door

Exit,
Gloomy and depressed,
To
Creaking frost
Which Sings
Squeakily
And
Stings
Cold toes.
Aargh!

But then
Ah!
When
I see
The optimistic green
Of emerging snowdrops
Some leaves
Bent
And crumbed
With defiant soil.

Ripe

That August
Was unusually hot
And over-ripe
With wasps
And stinging nettles.
Fruit
Torn from branches
Flowed on our tongues
Like warm kisses
As
We sauntered
Under
The ceaseless
Blue
Sky.

Really

Being anxious
Not to miss the rain
I took a long cut home.
Soon
The sound of water
Crushed and crashed
On water
Was
Like harpsichord music.
All around me
Cleansing rain
For a man
With a newly educated
Conscience
What was loyalty
Or
Stillborn
Words
Compared
With shifting flesh.

An Idea Jam

uneasy
Under the blue lighted
Nine o'clock moon
Ideas try to unfurl
And flap
Their brown wings
The rose pattern
On the carpet
Seems over-distinct today
Almost as though the blooms
Are in relief.
The thorns catching.
Flesh hurts against bones
And skin smarts.
Pale Picasso lights
Turn reddy grey
When filtered through
Clenched eyelids.

My throat
Is crudely
Dry
Sound is roughened
On its surface.
I can see blood drained fingers
Gripping a pencil
Which bends and snaps
The pieces
Clatter against the lampshade
Like ligneous moths.

Mill

At the end of the
alleyway
Hands rest on
sandstone
Which crumbles grittily
against skin.
I imagine the clatter of
clogs
As millhands
Scurry
Over the ringing bridge
To the mill
Which stands
As though it had
splintered
From crystalline rock
Rather than been built
Stone
Upon Stone.

Now the mill.
Is as empty
As a dead man's head.
Only rats remain
Like remnants
Of evil ideas.

Buzzard

Mile high
Flirting with a thermal
Wings steady
Tail angled
Dreaming
Perhaps
Or making meaning
Of far below movements.
How does it tell the difference
Between
A breeze motivated leaf
Or something
Of blood driven purpose?
What knowledge
Brings it
Crashing
With such sickening efficiency
To destroy
Without disturbing
A single feather?

The Second Coming

Well
How would I return?
The only certainty
Is
It must involve music.
A second Mozart
Would be too much to ask.
Perhaps it may be as a whale
Whose song is so perfect
That a whole ocean
Gathers to listen.
Maybe as a blackbird
Who makes dawn a joy
For all those it persuades from sleep.
Or
Perhaps
As just a simple syncopation
Of Balsam seeds
Rattling
On hard ground.

Need

I need her.
And moving from my bed
I see that the sun
Has gone and bruised the clouds.
Gilt framed
They gather and weep.
Outside
Beneath the tree
Is nothing but grass
And inside
A recollection
Ferocious
Beautiful
Fumbles
My mind.

Riverbank

By the riverbank
I pause and sit
Cattle
Black smudged on green
Feast
Whilst above them
Leaves shimmer.
A stone
Clops
Against bedrock.
The sound is fat
In the still air.
Downstream
Children
Shriek
And play away
The droning
Bee heavy
Day.

Suppose

Suppose
Just suppose
I lay my hand
Gently on yours
To experience
The feel of your flesh
And the provoking joy
Of your blood.
Suppose
Just suppose
I let my fingers
Flicker
To the luxury
Of your hair
And see
The flux of colours
As I slowly
Stroke
In the sunlight
And experience
The same shine
Swirling
In your eyes

Suppose
Just suppose
You dozed
With your hair
Splayed on my face
Your head
Gently on my shoulder
Your hot damp breath
Fingering my neck.
Suppose
Just
Suppose.

Raindrop

What a huge
Raindrop
Dangling
From a corrupted sunflower head.
Fatly
It wobbles
As if uncertain
Whether
To
Drop
Or
Not.
As it moves
Sunlight
Splits and reorganises
Again
And
Again
Pulsing areas of red
Tangles of green
Delights of yellow.

Then
It Drops
Swiftly
And glowingly
But becomes
Just
Transient
Green varnish
On a mossy stone.

Daydream

Sky
And clouds
And twigs
A crisscross
Of chaotic movement
Flexing twitching
Like provoked synapses
Splitting
Burning
Blue and white and grey
Maybe just shapes
In the frame.
But the immaculate blue
Stills
Then the white is gone
The grey sublimates
There's just calm
And a quietude of twigs.
Had it just been imagination
Like love
Expressed
By the uneven curve of
Flexed lips
And fathomless eyes.

Swallow

Swallow
Skim and skate
Knotting air to light
Blue
And amazing
Forage
The wind
For sustenance
Laying
Your dance on air
Like music.

Kestrel

In the evening
As light fades
A kestrel
Flutters
Black
Against the sky
Wingtips quivering.
Prey pinpointed.
It is utterly motionless
Poised to plunge
Driving
Flick-knife claws
At the delicate neck
Of its victim.
Afterwards
There is the silent
Spinning
Of a single
White feather
In the hushed air.

Alone

Stillness
Is tangible
Like a smell
Of stale air.
The old man sucks tea
Through his whiskers.
Something
Moves along a corridor.
On his table
Is a photograph
As brittle
And brown as his skin.
He dozes and dreams.
Upstairs
Below
On every side
Noise and people
Pass.

Possibility

Wind
Goads clouds
Across the sun
Causing
A multicolour
Frosted
Image
From a glass skylight
To move
Across their backs.
As they lay
As if by design
Each is
Fleshed
With the possibility
Of the other.

Oldness

Sunlight
Paled
By crystal foliage
Reveals
An old man
Whose limbs
Are sinewed with
Muscle
Like twisted rope.
His bones are sore
Within their skin bag
And his birds-wing
Breath
Disturbs
The air
Whitely.

If

If you
Should come
Through my door
Now
I would nearly
Smile
And say
Hi
Nice to see you
And inside remain
As still as boiling ice.
When your eyes
Looked around
At the unchanged
surroundings
I would stretch my lips
And say
Now what do you want
And recall
The glowing joy
Of your eyes,

The supernova shining
When you were glad.
I would wrinkle my Lips
or perhaps
Make a soothing
Gesture
With my hands
In recognition
Of the curve of your
hair.
An echo of its
gentleness
Somewhere
In my palm.

Bright Eyed Fox

Sneaky
In the long grass
Slinking fox
Keep the wind
Pinching
At your nose.
The fat rooster
Dreams
Squawking lazy
Pecking idly
Sun careless
Then
Snap
Teeth and raining feathers.
Run
As fast as a leaf
On a gale.
Only in your den
Can you stop
And snigger.

Another Swallow

Near the farmhouse
Swallows
Queued on the Gables
Chattering
And ready to fly
Towards
The September sun.
Others.
Perched aloof
On the beams
Of the tired barn,
Remained
Ready to die
In the first frosts of
winter.
It had been a good
year for swallows
Many had raised
A second brood

Footsteps

Footsteps
Sound
Endlessly
In the corridors of this
place
Footsteps
With the precision of
skin.
I know
That if I do not lower
this foot
I will never reach the
tree.
But branches beckon
On the breeze.
A sliver of sun light
Moves on the grass
Just as one
Had once done
Over her body.

Idle Moment

On the train
At last.
I stare
From the window
As seagulls
Grind out
Their regulation circles.
I doze
Then open one eye
And gaze
With the blue black
Lights of imagination
At a sudden smile.
Afterwards,
Walking slowly
In silent fog,
I watch her
Disappear
Into the rumbling dirty city.

Love

It was raining
And chimneys smoked
With a withering smell.
In the houses
People moved
In apparent peace.
As I walked past
I destroyed a rose head.
Smashed it with my fist.
Petals
Flew and showered.
Still with me
Smash
And petals erupted.
I could still sense
The tensions in her neck
As she struggled
Not to turn
As she walked
Away.

Autumn Snapshot

The September woodland
Is pine dense
But intruded by the occasional
Broadleaf tree.
Other pushy species
Are scarce,
Mainly shrivelled
And untroubled by light.
The soil is many shades of brown
But odd patches of sunlight
Flicker
A scant and random pattern
Dictated by the wind.
In the treetops
Sunlight
Strokes occasional leaves.
Brilliantly
Each favoured leaf
Glows transiently and shivers
As if stealthy autumn
Has made it insecure.

Owls

Nearly feathered
The owls sit
Playing the air
Raggedly
With half done wings.
Soon
Fully feathered
They will rake the
darkness
Using the black air
For their
Slick purposes.

Starling

In the corner of the farmyard
A pile of straw
Has blown high
Into the cup of the wall.
On top of the heap
Lays a
Shiningly spangled
Amazingly iridescent
Corpse
Of a starling.

Peacetalk

Yes!
That's all very well.
But what shape shall it be?
I know
How many died today
Give
Or take
A few thousand.
Never mind
Shall the table
Be round
Square
Oval
Oblong?
You've already moaned
Of the giggling
Skulls
Bobbing
In the swamps.
No matter!
The main issue is

Dare
We allow it to be
Kidney shaped?
No!
Don't be silly my dear good man
Because
There is no advantage
To be gained
By including a culvert
Along which
Blood can gurgle and drain.
No!
Today we must decide
Whether
We dare concede
A red tablecloth
Or
Who Is to sit where
And
On what.

Viaduct

From a viaduct
A hundred feet
Above the river
Nothing is heard
Of any
Dialogue
Between
Water and rock.
Along the catwalk
Boltholes
Punctuate
Weathered metal.
Through them
Far below
You can see
Trees which sway
Like Scheherazade
For the Zsar
And hold up
A clatter of crow
And knotted twig.

On either side
Parapets
Latticed and grey
Play
Tin whistle
Tunes
Arranged by wind.

Removal Day

Tinkle whistle
Tinkle whistle
The sound spreads
From egg to egg.
The goose returns
And squats
Vastly damp
On the warm
Down covered
Worlds.
And still
Like naughty children
Talking after lights out
Egg
Speaks to
Egg
Arranging removal day.
Go faster
Go slower
Steady now
Ready now

Knock
Knock
Chip chip
Crack!
A noise out of all proportion
And the small
Acorn coloured beaks
Thrust out
Into the damp feathered air.

Tarn

The surface
Is textured by wind
Tearing patterns
Across the water.
Who would have thought that rock
So solid and enduring
Could shift as frailly.
As a broken shadow.

Dawn Realisation

Opened eyes
And saw
The solitary star.
No
Not star
But
Planet
Venus
Like Wordsworth's
Friendless violet
Alone
In eloquent
Monologue.
Alone like me
Once I feared that I alone
Am
Alone
But
Now
I know it.

Shoes

The deadest
Thing I know
Is a dead man's shoes.
Tossed on the floor
One on its side
Tongue still
Laces trailing
Like black worms
With glittery eyes.
The toecaps reflect care
And forethought
But they lie
Still as no breath
Nobodies
Now.

How Irrational

How irrational is
The power to please
A cadence of notes
Just so
Like the curve
Of a willing smile
A streak
Of paint
Bristle twisted
Just so
To be pretend fabric
On a curving breast.
A spectacularly appropriate word
Just so
Creating more
Than the image desired
Like an eye
Glistening
And surprised
By love.

The Gala

They've getten
A nice day for it.
Poom pa poom
Pa Pa poom
The sound seems to
Stick
In the clouds which
Shimmer and fade
Into grey blue
Uncertainty.
Pom Pa Poom Pa
Poom
Closer now
The beat stricter
And there they are.
Clotted clouds
condense
In the shine of the
instruments.
Purple orange twirling
greys
Mine into the surface.

The march of glory
Faded now
Progressed to another
And perhaps woeful
fate.
Poom
Pa
Poom
Pa
Poom.

It Was an Instant

It was an instant
Where breath
Stopped.
If you don't believe
That love can do this
Then think again.
I suppose
Time paused
For viewer
And viewed.
Mutual acknowledgement
Of the moment.
Then the spinning
Spate
Resumed
And
Some might think
That nothing had
Irrevocably
Changed.

Raging

Raging
Against
The dying light
Is all very well
Dylan
But
All it does
Is pile anxiety on agony
Or even agony on anxiety
Move on to
Dust
Gracefully
Like a burnished leaf
Running on a
Sunset breeze.

One Step Further

Just
When you think
You
Can't go another step.
Just when your
Rasping breath
Pauses
In a spasm
In your side.
You clear the ridge
And somehow
Breathing
Becomes unimportant
As
Shadows of clouds
Pursue
One another
Across
The sun scoured
Valley bottom.

Firebird

The colours
Chagall pinks and blues
Flicker
Among the parting leaves.
Who would have thought
That pink fire could release
So much blue
In the dancing water
Around her
Twirling feathers.
At last
Free In the water
She turns
And her fire
Is in kaleidoscopic rings of
Gold
And green
And blue
On and on
Like ascending notes
Like loves ending
Where you beg
Don't stop
Don't ever stop
Don't.

Approaching Storm

Sudden wind
And
It is as if
The rock
Had stealthily fumbled on
A grey cloak.
Closely and harshly
The abrupt rain
Tramples
The blue waved water.
It is rinsed grey.
Reflections are tumbled
In misty windy cloudiness.
Boats
Still move
But silently now
As though they had
Become ghosts
Their wash
Spectral white
In the gloom.

A raven
Saws
Its call
From a rock
As if angry
That flight was
Suspended.

A Sudden Gust

Ginger bracken
Like misplaced hair
From the head of a bald man
Wavers in the whipped water.
Rocks smashed
Into a million twisted pieces
Create
An impossible puzzle.
Then
The shrieking stops.
Just as though
Someone
Had slammed a door.
Now you can hear
The tapping
Of the lapping water
On the lakeshore
As gradually
The pieces reassemble
To reflected reality.

Heron

Somehow
The heron
Steps
Like an awkward ballerina
Without
Disturbing the water.
Even the sunlight
Seems
To have less
Effect on the surface beneath it.
Then it spreads its wings
Like a priest's cloak
Forming a shroud of darkness
For the glinting fish's
Last moment.

Anger

Only your eyes
Let everyone know
You do understand
Your problem
Even though your words provoke
As they grate
Like rock on rock
On the seashore
Whilst you fold your arms
Grasping the impossibility
Of the situation
And hug yourself
As the syllables
Tumble and grind
Nowhere describing
Anything
Near
Your
Thoughts
Or needs.

Stormy Jackdaw

The damned daft jackdaw
Twitchy
On a jittery twig
Flicks his head
From side to side.
Perplexed
It raises
One set of frozen claws
And
Flurries snow onto the ground.
It flies
In its own
Outburst of snow
To the shed roof
And wallows
Wings
Beating
Wildly
In its own storm.

Brief Encounter

The slate walls
Were head high
And grey
As the ashen sky.
Mud
Lined the stony chasm
And tugged our boots
At every step.
Then there were sounds
Like too quick slithering footfalls
And a musk.
A badger
Perhaps.
We stopped
Stilled with hope
Clutching our picnic
In blued fingers.
Then round the bend she came
Large black spots on her body
Snout
Spreading misty rhythmic plumes
Of steam.
A Gloucester Old Spot.

She paused
And we passed the time of day
Politely
Shared a slice of Christmas cake
Then
We all went our wet way.

Bird On a Rock

The sand
Spread
Crinkles
In recollection
Of the tides pattern
Whilst
Along the beating
Waters edge
A bulging
Rumpled
Carroty sun
Flushed
The sand
With gilt paint.
Then I saw it,
The bird on a rock,
Like
A painted target
On a fairground stall.
Metallic
Catching
Collecting
Reflecting
The last rays of brightness.

I expected it
To turn
Mechanically with a flick
And a click
To face its doom.
But no
All remained breathlessly still
At the turning point
It stood
Motionless
Like a photograph
Of itself.

The Nettle

Just the wariest touch
In passing
And yet
White pain
Tingles in my fingers.
I flick them
Agitatedly
Swearing
Then suck them
Noisily.
I think
Of trampling
The wretched plant
Into the ground
But
Then the late sun
Slips
From behind
A gold edged cloud.
The leaves
Appear to harden
Like metal.
Tooth edged like cogs
On asymmetric wheels.

It is no longer possible
To covet revenge
But
Just to admire
With my fingers
Tracing
The saw tooth shapes
In the warm air.

What Is It

What is it about a church?
The emphatic clonk
Of the pitted latch.
The protracted wail
Of the hinges
As the massive door swings.
The echoing shot
Of the closure
As you are trapped
In abrupt calmness.
Then the soothing of air
As peace grips.
Carefully
You control your breathing
So as not to disturb
Anything at all
And walk with measured step
Through the praying wood
And the crystallised Light.

Yesterday

Yesterday
The wood anemones
Flashed
As though
Charged
With white energy
But today
Unexpectedly
Thanks to a sudden
Blooming
Extravagance of greenness
And sun
The petals
Seem subtly
Limed
With cooler light.

A Giggle of Water

A laughter of water
Among the resounding rocks
Writes a picture in bubbles
Disturbing
The fallen depiction
Of the clouds and sky.
The images are
Fractured
Like reflections
Of my
Disturbance
At
Our
Last
Parting.

The Ruthless Water

The ruthless water
Has scoured the bones
Dead white.
The angled skull
Gushes tears
Maybe forever.
Just the odd rib remains
And a thighbone.
Compassion
Was never relevant
To this situation
Only certainty.

Spider

What a priceless
Creation
Set
On strands
Of purest crystal
Turned to flame by the rising sun.
Eight steely pillars
Of seeming endless strength
Support
A sphere around which
Eyes blink
Like garnets
As it
Relentlessly
Seeks
Prey.

Funny

No not really
How pain
Throbs my time to
Its fulfilment.
Strange
No not strange
How rigidity
As a state of mind
Firms
In the frail flesh.
Ridiculous
No not ridiculous
That the word
Was six
And not sex
And the question
Can I have
Coming from your lips
Now
Should never have
Astounded.

Glorious

It was glorious
In its joy
With a tall svelte stem
Ribbed to infinity
Leaves
Which turned
To relish the light
And petals of such yellow
That the sun
Must have been
Jealous.
Now
The petals have tumbled
And soon become
Browned
As one
With the soil.

Leaves are dry and twisted
And seem to point
Accusingly
At the grey rain filled sky.
It is glorious
But worrying
In its
Submission.

Oyster Catcher

Like a demented referee
The Oyster catcher
Signals hysterically
As though its authority
Over the land
Was suddenly
And devastatingly
Challenged.
The nearby stream
Seems
To discuss
The disturbance
With the stones
Playing its quiet notes
Calling gently but urgently
For peace.
Higher and higher
More Frenzied
The cacophony continues
Even though I was then in the next
field.
It would seem
The matter had become
A grudge.

Leaf Fall

A withering wind
Worries
Orange wrinkled leaves
And dislodges
Just
One,
It twizzles in the air
Like an
Out of control
Butterfly.
Then flicks upside down
Spilling crystal
Dewdrops.
Which sing
Colour.
I stretch for it
But
Somehow
Like an elusive idea
It evades
Even a touch
And
Settles
To the stony ground.

In The Footsteps

I follow the footsteps of
William and Dorothy.
Whoosh!
Pssst!
Whoosh!
Whoosh!
Pssst!
Whoosh!
Doppler arranges
The passing sound
Again and again.
So much angry air.
But where I am
I need to think past it.
I stand and see water
Jigging
Over maybe
The same stones
That
They
Stood on.

Perhaps there was
The same slurping sound
When they looked
And saw
That their
Indented boot-prints
Were burnished with rising water.
In the mud
On the bankside
Around me
The wind
Strokes the trees.
Branches gently bend
In shaking curves
Of salutation
Whilst below
The daffodils
Tilt and reel
As if bending their heads
In excited conversation
About the ways
Sun and water
Flicker and shine.

The Grey Room

Inside the room,
Trapped
In a wicked chair
I heard the music drone.
Outside,
An apple tree
Fruitful
But dull
Seemed subdued
With shivering
Damp leaves
As if they had become
Too much of a burden.
Impulsive sunlight
Smashed the clouds
And
The tree dazzled
With astonishing colour.
A sudden
Squabbling of jackdaws
A bubbling of birds
Boiled
Around the fruit

All too soon
They evaporated
As clouds
Smothered the sunlight.
Inside the room
Trapped on a wicked chair
The grey music droned.

Seascape

From the clifftop
You could hear
The sea
Sing slowly
With a mellow
Reassuring breath.
As if that was not enough
A form flowing in white
Arrived and danced
On the shoreline.
Her movements
Were like petals
Twirling
Gently
And sympathetically
In the breeze.
I turned aside
For just a second
But she was gone,
Vanished,
Only the seas
Capering rhythm
Remained
As celebration
Of her presence.

Bean Sprout

Strange
How the first
Brutal green eruption
Of the spiralling bean shoot
Changes
The urgency of my breathing.
Allegedly
Just
Because
There is something of
Joy about it.
Yet
Why so
We both
Live
With the same
Inconsequential
And
Bitter
Inevitability.

The Autumn Wind

The wind
Is aggressive.
Its noise
A grouchy non-tune
Braying
Set to a syncopation
Of drumming twigs.
The wind
Is hostile.
It slams the rain
With such vigour against the window
And yet
The downflow of drops
Is gentle
And unsteady
Like the waddling walk of an old
man.

The wind
Is belligerent
Beating the soil
And water
To a muddy bubbling froth
The rising Misty spray
Smells
Like drying boots
Beside a fire.

Sense Of Direction

Like a demented signpost
The stubborn remains
Of the
Bark-free Shine-free tree
Stick rigidly to their decision.
One branch invites you
To visit a grey black cloud
With a golden edge
Of trapped sunlight.
Or there again another
Suggests
A breathless journey
To the pike top
With its fierce edge
Cutting the sky
From the blasted rock.
Another insistent limb
Points to the grass
Where speedwell
Has scooped and magnified
Blueness
Which appears to stretch
To the edge of space.

Yet another
Points
Accusingly
To a whole tree
Whose leaves tremble
As if in memory
Of just one seed.
The final finger
Broken
But firm
Aims
Straight above
To where God
Allegedly is.

The Power Shovel

The mechanical shovel
Rhythmically
Brayed the earth
Into submission,
Wallop
Wallop
Wallop!
Soil was clanked
To a thudding shivering lorry
Each bucketful
Nearly a seismic event.
Someone drove nails
Into stunned wood
Boom
Boom
Blast!
Raised voices
With
Scalpel edged penetration
Were like
A chorus of cats.
One man bellowed
An unrecognisable song.
Another whistled
Discordantly.
Then

Unexpectedly
There was just
The ticking
Of cooling machinery
And the eccentric
Fussing
Of a solitary wood pigeon.
A group swig
Thermos violated coffee
And banter.
One
On the thin red line
Ate powerfully.
Another peed
At the remaining
Un-grubbed hedge
Leaves vibrating
And steaming
Enthusiastically
Whilst
The pigeon
Continued
Its
Surprised
Comment.

Things

Things on which we pin
Existence.
Things
That in a way
Store
Actuality
In a fragile
Unreal
Tinsel cage.
A ring on a finger
Swollen and bent
Which
Twists and locks
Unexpectedly.
A cup from someone
Never forgotten
Used in preference.
China
Through which
You can see
The tremble
Of coffee
As your hand shakes.

A watch
Seldom wound
Filigreed with silver
Like frost
On a windowpane.
Just things.
Someone's treasure
Someone's realisation of a few
pence
Someone's
Trash.

Ninth Symphony

How to contain
So
Much
Latent anger
Without shedding blood.
The assertive drumming
Insisting
There
Are
Good
Grounds
For Fury
Whilst
The strings
Urge tranquillity
And joy
Of sheer achievement.
But no
Crack the drums
Citing life's unfairness
The me
Being
The all
With a pounding
Of blurred
Vibration

Until finally
The shaking
Of a fist
Against
The
Strike of lightning
And the beating thunder.

The Dance

For a short while
The silence is mesmeric.
At that time I swear
You can even hear
The dance of
The thrush's feet
On the lawn
Before the worm's
Final stretched surrender.
A blackbird
On the top of the shed door
Cleans its beak,
Bone grating on wood
Scrape
Scrape
Scrape
Its body swaying
Rock
Twist
Roll
As though
Asking for entry
To the dance.

A curlew
In the distance
Gently rehearses its flute
To a crescendo
As if
Confident
It too would be welcome
To the same party.

Meteor

A sun churns
And boils
with soundless anger
Struggling
With maniacal strength
To maintain its integrity.
Flames
Like grasping fingers
Shoot a million miles
Through space
As though appealing
For the reversal
Of the inevitable.
Soon the floundering mass
Contracts and contracts
But brightens
As it goes
Until its incandescence
Outshines a galaxy.
Silently it disintegrates.
Molten rocks
Some the size of a planet
Some like wobbly pebbles
Are spat

In soundless fire
From the heart of the
Exploding star.
Twirling and spinning
One homeless rock
Immediately cold
Flies
Over millions and millions
Of miles of emptiness
Perhaps to fly forever.
But
At last,
It feels a wrench.
And earthly fire polishes it
Eye black.
Now it sits.
Marbled and marvellous
Nearly at journeys end.
Only anther 5 billion years
To resume its quest.

A Moment of Peace

It's good
To be sitting here
Doing nothing
A prisoner from work.
Around me
The captive flower heads
Finger the breeze
Gently
So as not to disturb
Anything.
Nearby
The tumbled shed
Is warmly neglected
Jobs abandoned.
Motes
Of gemstone dust
Float indolently in a sunbeam.
A trowel idles in a corner
Naturally never thinking
Of planting the abandoned Cosmos.
The tap drowsily drips
The drops wobble
Stealthily in the air
And hiccup
Almost silently
As they spread-eagle on the floor

As if apologising for the disturbance.
So
Why not
Grasp this moment
As the stilled bombs
Are about
To mushroom.

© Ray Lee 2025

ISBN: 978-1-918038-26-2

www.ingramcontent.com/pod-product-compliance
Lightning Source LLC
Chambersburg PA
CBHW052052070526
44584CB00017B/2143